The Akashi Kaikyo Bridge

by Kaye Patchett

BLACKBIRCH PRESS

An imprint of Thomson Gale, a part of The Thomson Corporation

Detroit • New York • San Francisco • San Diego • New Haven, Conn. • Waterville, Maine • London • Munich

For more information, contact
Blackbirch Press
27500 Drake Rd.
Farmington Hills, MI 48331–3535
Or you can visit our Internet site at http://www.gale.com

Photo credits: cover © Kaku Kurita/Time Life Pictures/Getty Images; page 4 Kyodo/Landov; page 8 Oliver Strewe/Lonely Planet Images; pages 10, 12, 20 Photos.com; page 11 © Michael S. Yamashita/CORBIS; page 14 Martin Moos/Lonely Planet Images; page 16 © Robert Essel NYC/CORBIS; page 22 © CORBIS; pages 23, 24, 26, 28, 31, 33, 39 Honshu–Shikoku Bridge Authority; page 34 Kimimasa Mayama/Reuters/Landov; page 36 © Taxi by Getty Images; pages 40, 43 © Simon Charles Rowe/Lonely Planet Images; page 44 © Royalty–Free/CORBIS

LIBRARY OF CONGRESS CATALOGING–IN–PUBLICATION DATA

Patchett, Kaye.
 The Akashi Kaikyo Bridge / by Kaye Patchett.
   p. cm. — (Building world landmarks)
  ISBN 1–4103–0140–0 (hardback)
 Summary: Discusses the construction of the Akashi Kaikyo Bridge in Japan.
  1. Akashi Kaikyo Ohashi (Kobe–shi, Japan)—History—Juvenile literature. I. Title. II. Series.

  TG106.K63P38 2004
  624.2'3'0952187—dc22   2004007269

Printed in the United States
10 9 8 7 6 5 4 3 2 1

Table of Contents

A Much-Needed Connection

THE NATION OF Japan consists of four main islands and three to four thousand smaller ones. Honshu, the largest main island, is neighbored by Hokkaido to the north and Kyushu to the south. Shikoku, the smallest main island, lies alongside the southeastern shore of Honshu, across the Seto Inland Sea. Between the two lies tiny Awaji Island.

This natural separation had always posed a major challenge for transportation. Honshu was connected to Kyushu by two railway tunnels beneath the Kanmon Strait in 1942 and 1944. A road tunnel was added in 1958, and a bridge in 1973. A high-speed rail tunnel in 1975 completed the series of links between Honshu and Kyushu. The Seikan rail tunnel connects Honshu with Hokkaido. Construction started in 1964 and the tunnel opened in 1988.

Opposite:
The Akashi Kaikyo Bridge, an astounding feat of engineering, is the world's longest and tallest suspension bridge.

Shikoku, however, remained isolated. People could travel from Honshu to Shikoku by ferry, but Japan experiences some of the most extreme weather conditions in the world. Violent typhoon winds often make ferry travel dangerous and unreliable.

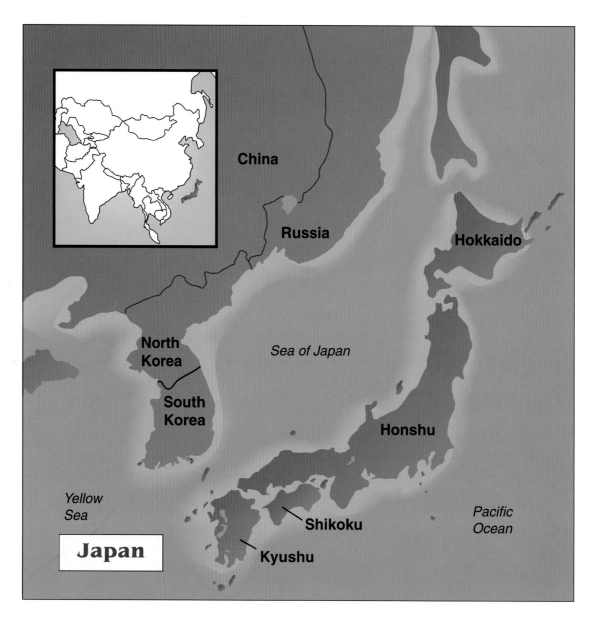

The Akashi Kaikyo Bridge, opened in 1998, was part of the solution to this problem. Also called the Pearl Bridge, it is the star feature of a gigantic national road project that has built three separate crossings between Honshu and Shikoku. The bridge is part of a safe, fast, and convenient route that connects Honshu, home of Japan's biggest and busiest cities, with the formerly isolated and underdeveloped islands of Awaji and Shikoku.

The nearly two-and-a-half-mile-long Akashi Kaikyo Bridge is the world's longest and tallest suspension bridge. It stretches 12,831 feet (3,911 m) from Honshu to Awaji Island, across the Akashi Strait, or kaikyo. Its center span of 6,532 feet (1,991 m) is longer than five Empire State Buildings laid end to end. The span is 1,906 feet (581 m) longer than that of Britain's Humber Bridge, the previous record holder, and almost a quarter-mile (367 m) longer than Denmark's Storebaelt Bridge, also opened in 1998. The Akashi Kaikyo Bridge towers are 928 feet (283 m) high—almost as tall as the Eiffel Tower. The bridge is also the most expensive bridge ever built. It cost about 500 billion Japanese yen, or about 4.3 billion U.S. dollars.

Chapter 1

Journey to Modern Times

UNTIL THE MID 1800s, Japan was isolated from the rest of the world. The nation had been closed to foreigners for more than 250 years, but in 1853, American captain Matthew Perry sailed to Japan and asked that trade be resumed. Foreign relations were reestablished, and modernization followed rapidly. A modern military and a two-house parliament replaced the rule of shoguns and samurai warriors. A telegraph system and a railroad network were built, but travel between the nation's many islands was an obstacle yet to be overcome.

In 1889 a local government official named Jinnojo Okubo suggested that bridges be built to connect the islands of Honshu and Shikoku. He had no technical plan for how the bridges could be built, however, and so his idea went no further. In 1916 Toranosuke Nakagawa, a

Opposite:
The Akashi Kaikyo Bridge helps connect the island of Honshu with the once isolated island of Shikoku.

After the Golden Gate Bridge (pictured) was built in San Francisco, Japanese engineers suggested a similar bridge could be built across the Naruto Strait.

senator, put forward a proposal to the National Diet, or Japanese legislature, for a bridge link between the two islands. Like Okubo twenty-seven years earlier, he had no plan for how the bridges—one of which would need to be almost two-and-a-half-miles (4,023 m) long—could be built across the Seto Inland Sea. The technology simply did not exist.

The matter rested until 1940, when a government public works manager named Chujiro Haraguchi offered the first technical plan. He had studied the Golden Gate Bridge, built in California in 1937, and suggested Japan could build a similar bridge between Shikoku and Awaji Island, across the Naruto Strait. Combined with a ferry from Awaji Island to Honshu, the bridge would reduce travel time between the two main islands and make the crossing safer. His plan was welcomed, but it seemed the project was not to be. World War II intervened, and construction plans came to a halt.

When the war ended, plans to bridge the Seto Inland Sea were put aside while Japan faced the enormous task of rebuilding entire cities leveled by bombing.

The Road Link Revisited

After the war, new factories and new technology opened the way for Japan to become a modern industrial nation. On Honshu, big cities such as Tokyo and Kobe flourished, but the people of Shikoku were hampered. They could not rely on ferries to export goods such as fresh foods to Honshu and other parts of Japan, because fog and ferocious winds often made the Seto Inland Sea impassable. Honshu and Kyushu had been joined by a railroad tunnel in 1942, and in 1946 preliminary studies were begun for a rail tunnel between Honshu and Hokkaido. Modern travel between three of the four main islands was provided

Before the Akashi Kaikyo Bridge was built, residents of Shikoku villages like this one faced a dangerous journey across the Seto Inland Sea to Honshu.

Suspension Bridges

Suspension bridges have been used for thousands of years. Some, still used in India, China, and South America to span deep gorges, consist simply of two ropes—one to walk on and another to hold on to. More advanced versions have a bamboo or plank roadway, suspended by hangers from rope cables.

The first suspension bridge to use a road deck stiffened with trusses was built by James Finley across Jacob's Creek, Pennsylvania, in 1801. It was sixty-nine feet (21 m) long and used iron chains for cables. In the late nineteenth century, mass production of steel revolutionized bridge construction. Stronger than iron, steel heralded new advances in long-span bridge technology. John Roebling's 3,460-foot-long (1,055 m) Brooklyn Bridge, completed in 1883, was the longest suspension bridge in the world. Roebling was the first to use steel wires for bridge suspension cables.

The cables of modern suspension bridges are up to several feet thick and are made from individual steel wires compressed into a strand that can hold thousands of tons in weight. The cables support the road deck and are secured

On a suspension bridge, the roadway is suspended from huge main cables that extend from one end of the bridge to the other.

to anchorages on shore. The anchorages resist the sideways pull from the cables, while the towers and their foundations support the vertical load.

Wind can be dangerous to suspension bridges, as the designers of the Tacoma Narrows Bridge across Puget Sound discovered on November 7, 1940. Waves of motion caused by a forty-two-mile-per-hour (67 km) wind caused the light, narrow deck to writhe, twist, and then tear itself apart. Today, engineers strengthen bridges with steel trusses and use wind-tunnel tests to ensure that the disaster that engulfed "Galloping Gertie" could not recur.

for, but Shikoku remained isolated by the ocean, as it had been for thousands of years.

In May 1955 two ferries collided and sank between Honshu and Shikoku. Many of the 168 people who drowned were middle school students on an excursion. The tragedy highlighted the urgent need for a bridge, and both the national and local governments began to research how to make the project possible.

Since his 1940 proposal to build a suspension bridge across part of the Seto Inland Sea, Haraguchi had become mayor of Kobe. He expanded his original ideal and now suggested that two huge bridges be built: one across the Naruto Strait from Shikoku to Awaji, and another across the Akashi Strait between Awaji and Kobe. It would be a colossal project, but the proposition came at the right time. In 1950 the government had passed the National Land Comprehensive Development Law to encourage development of remote parts of the country. Its aim was to spread economic growth across the whole nation. In 1953 the Remote Island Development Act was enacted to promote the development of Japan's smallest islands.

As a part of this national enterprise, studies were set in motion by the Japan National Railway and the Japanese Ministry of Construction to decide whether a system of rail and highway links to the island of Shikoku would be practical. They passed their results on to the Japan Society of Civil Engineers, which formed a technical committee to carry out more detailed studies. In 1967 the committee presented its final report in favor of the project. Although a bridge across the Akashi Strait would be longer than any span ever constructed, Japan's top engineers agreed it could be built.

A Gigantic Project

The government approved the giant road project, but the program was simply too enormous for the Ministry of Transportation to supervise. A project of such magnitude needed a department all its own. On July 1, 1970, the Honshu-Shikoku Bridge Authority was created to plan and construct three separate highway routes across the Seto Inland Sea. It would be one of the biggest public works projects ever undertaken and would comprise more than 116 miles (187 km) of highway and a total of eighteen long–span bridges to connect a scattering of tiny islands that lie like stepping stones between Honshu and Shikoku.

The almost three-decades-long enterprise was carried out in stages. The bridge authority conducted

The Seto Ohashi Bridge is a series of bridges spanning the Seto Inland Sea between the islands of Honshu and Shikoku.

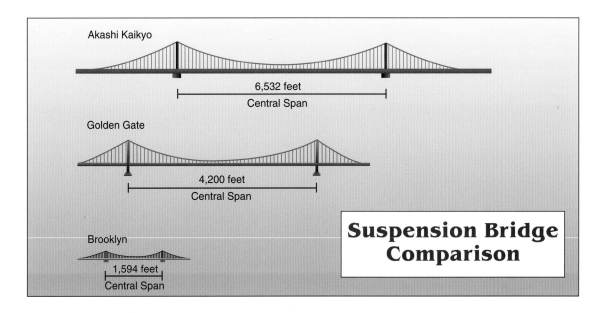

Akashi Kaikyo

6,532 feet
Central Span

Golden Gate

4,200 feet
Central Span

Brooklyn

1,594 feet
Central Span

Suspension Bridge Comparison

cost estimates and authorized weather studies to ensure that the structures to be built would be able to withstand the strongest possible winds. Engineers explored ways to excavate the seabed and investigated the strengths and weaknesses of long-span bridges.

The crowning achievement of the project would be the nearly two-and-a-half-mile (3,911 km) Akashi Kaikyo Bridge. It would be the longest bridge on the planet—almost twice as long as Japan's longest suspension bridges. The original plan for the bridge included a railroad track, but after some thought the government abandoned the idea to run trains on the bridge. Plans for the Akashi Kaikyo Bridge were put on hold. In 1985 officials decided to redesign it as a highway bridge, and in April 1986 ground was officially broken for the record-breaking structure. Although actual construction did not start until May 1988, work on the longest bridge in the world had begun.

A World-Class Challenge

UNLIKE MANY OF the world's famous bridges, which were the work of a single, brilliant engineer—such as John Roebling's Brooklyn Bridge or John Rennie's London Bridge—the Akashi Kaikyo Bridge was a team effort of an entire nation. Four hundred engineers from the Honshu-Shikoku Bridge Authority and hundreds of engineers from universities and private companies all contributed to its design. From design to completion, more than 2 million people took part in the project. The actual task of construction was so immense, it had to be broken down into separate stages and divided among more than one hundred contractors.

The people who designed the world's longest bridge faced a world-class engineering challenge. The Akashi Kaikyo Bridge would be built in a location subject to

Opposite:
The deep water of the Akashi Strait was one of many challenges engineers faced in designing the bridge.

major earthquakes, tsunamis, and typhoon winds. Its structure would need enough strength and flexibility to stand firm against an earthquake with a magnitude of 8.5 on the Richter scale and to withstand winds of 180 miles (290 km) per hour. The bridge would be constructed in waters up to 361 feet (110 m) deep, with strong tidal currents of 15 feet (4.5 m) per second. More than fourteen hundred ships pass through the Akashi Strait every day, and construction would be further complicated by the need to keep the channel open at all times.

Firm Foundations

The bridge's two towers would stand nearly one and one quarter miles (2 km) apart, on either side of the deepest part of the strait. This would keep the deep center channel clear for ships to pass through safely. The towers would stand far enough to the sides of the busy channel that there would be no danger that a ship might collide with one of them. Thick twin cables laid over saddles at the top of the towers would transmit the bridge's 120,000-ton weight to its foundations.

The weight of a suspension bridge is supported by anchorages in addition to towers. Two huge concrete anchorages would be built, one on each shore, to anchor the bridge's cables firmly at each end. The importance of solid anchorages can be illustrated by imagining two upright pencils joined by a length of string, which represent the towers and cables of a suspension bridge. A heavy weight attached to the center of the string would cause the pencils to fall over at once; but if the string was extended and attached to a strongly anchored block at either end, the pencils would hold firm even when the string was pressed heavily downward. The anchorages for the Akashi Kaikyo Bridge would be the largest in the world, weighing 350,000 and 370,000 tons.

To form a solid foundation for the towers, two immense steel caissons would be sunk onto the pre-excavated seabed and filled with special underwater cement. Caissons are cylindrical shells that form an outer case for underwater foundations. The two caissons for

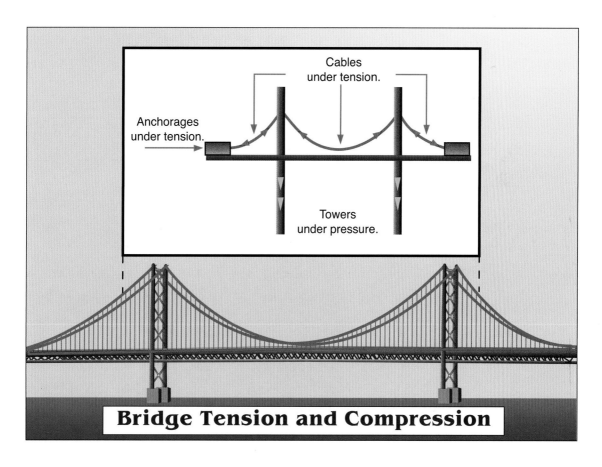

Anchorages under tension.

Cables under tension.

Towers under pressure.

Bridge Tension and Compression

Tension and Compression

Tension and compression forces operate in every structure, from bridges to buildings. Tension stretches things and will pull them apart if it is too great, while compression presses things together. Ropes and cables are very strong in tension. Stone has great compressive strength but will crack under tension.

A simple bridge made from a wooden plank might safely support one or two people, but a heavy weight would break it. This is because the top of the plank is in compression, while the lower surface is in tension. As the underside stretches in response to the heavy pressure on top, the plank bends and finally snaps apart with a loud crack. The sound is the result of the material springing back into place as the tension is released.

Trusses are used to strengthen bridge structures because they separate the forces of tension and compression. A truss consists of an upper and lower beam connected by a series of triangles. The triangle supplies stiffness because, unlike a square or rectangle, its shape changes hardly at all under pressure.

Stone arch bridges are in compression and are very strong. When a heavy vehicle crosses an arch bridge, compressive forces are directed downward and outward through the wedges of stone that compose the arch and into the supporting piers.

A suspension bridge is similar to an inverted arch. The weight of the bridge deck is carried upward to the curved cables. The cables, which are in tension, carry the weight to the anchorages. At the same time, compressive forces press downward on the towers, to transmit weight to the foundations.

Stone arch bridges are very strong because the load of the bridge is distributed outward, along the curve of the arch.

the Akashi Kaikyo Bridge would be the biggest ever made: about 262 feet (80 m) in diameter and 230 feet (70 m) in height—as high as a thirty-three-story building.

Wind Tunnel Testing

When the foundations and towers were in place, hanger cables would be attached to the main cables to support the road deck. The deck would be stiffened by steel trusses. A truss is a long supporting frame made of connected triangles. It helps make a bridge aerodynamically stable, because the open triangles allow wind to blow through. A solid surface would resist wind, as a sail does, and cause a bridge to sway dangerously.

In long-span bridges, aerodynamic stability is a must. The Akashi Kaikyo Bridge's long center span would make it especially vulnerable to damage from strong winds. To test how the structure would behave under typhoon-strength winds, the bridge authority ordered a huge wind tunnel to be built. Inside the tunnel, they placed a scale model one hundred times smaller than the bridge. The wind tunnel tests showed that the tower tops would vibrate if winds swirled rapidly around them. To combat this problem, engineers decided to install pendulum-like devices, called tuned mass dampers, inside the towers. If the bridge started to sway due to wind or an earthquake, the weight of the mass dampers would move in the opposite direction to prevent, or damp, the motion.

The wind tunnel tests also revealed the need for vertical stabilizing fins, or plates, to be installed below

A scale model of the Akashi Kaikyo Bridge was tested in a huge wind tunnel like this one to make sure that the long center span would be able to withstand strong winds.

the center of the road deck, together with an open grating along the length of the bridge. The plates would direct the wind flow above and below the road deck, equalizing the air pressure. If the air pressure on either surface of a bridge deck is greater than the pressure on the other surface, destructive waves of motion, called galloping, can form. A similar effect can be created with a jump rope: If two people hold either end and one moves the rope up and down, waves form along the length of the rope. Triggered by certain

Caissons

Caissons are huge cylindrical or box-shaped structures used to construct underwater foundations. Floating caissons are used for piers, breakwaters, or bridge foundations. They are made in a factory from steel, reinforced concrete, or wood, then floated to the site and sunk onto foundations on the seabed. Lastly, the inside of the caissons is filled with concrete. Open caissons are used in shallow water or on the shore. They are open at both ends and have a sharp edge that cuts into the soft ground below. As the mud and silt inside is dredged out with pipes, the caisson sinks lower and sec-

A caisson is towed into place to be used as part of the underwater foundation of the Akashi Kaikyo Bridge.

tions are added to the top. When the caisson reaches solid ground, it is filled with concrete to form a strong, deep foundation for bridge abutments.

Pneumatic caissons are used to dig deep underwater foundations. Invented in England in the 1850s, they have a sealed, pressurized chamber at the bottom for workers. James Buchanan Eads used pneumatic caissons to dig pier foundations for the Eads Bridge across the Mississippi River at St. Louis, which was completed in 1874. As the caisson sank deeper, the air pressure was increased to keep out water. However, workers began to get a strange disease after they climbed back out. They called it "caisson disease," or "the bends." The disease caused intense pain, nausea, and sometimes death. Years later, doctors discovered the reason for the condition. When workers returned too quickly from high to normal air pressure, nitrogen bubbles formed in their bloodstream, like fizz from a soda bottle, and lodged in their joints or veins. Nowadays, caisson workers and divers return from high pressure in stages, which allows extra nitrogen to be released gradually and safely.

Each of the fifteen-thousand-ton caissons was sunk in almost two hundred feet of water, with their tops visible above the water's surface.

changes in wind pressure, galloping can make a light, narrow road deck heave violently in gigantic ripples until it literally tears itself apart.

Construction Begins

Before the enormous bridge could be built, the bridge authority studied the geology of the strait and surrounding area. The seabed consisted of gravel and smaller particles above a layer of soft rocks composed mainly of sandstone. Granite, an extremely hard rock, lay beneath the Awaji shore. Site work began in May 1988 to prepare the seabed for placement of the fifteen-thousand-ton caissons that would support the towers.

To make an even surface on which to place the caissons, workers used huge buckets mounted on barges to scoop out nearly 19.5 million cubic feet (550,000 cu. m) of dirt and rock in wet, one-hundred-ton mouthfuls.

They dug flat-bottomed holes about forty-six feet (14 m) deep and as big as a baseball field. In mid-1989, twelve tugboats towed each caisson to its site, where it would be sunk into place in 197 feet (60 m) of water, on either side of the deepest part of the strait.

To sink the caissons, workers first anchored them in place and then gradually filled their hollow outer walls, which were divided into sixteen 39-foot-wide (12 m) compartments, with water. With the aid of instruments to monitor their position, the caissons came to rest within one inch (25 mm) of their planned locations, their tops visible above the surface of the water.

Net bags filled with gravel were placed around the base of each caisson, and one-ton rocks were laid on the seabed at a distance of twice the radius of the caissons to prevent the ocean floor around them from being washed away by the strong tidal currents. After the caissons were sunk, workers used a pipe to suck out debris and loose dirt from the central compartments, which opened directly onto the seabed.

Next workers filled the center of the caissons with concrete, like giant gelatin molds. A special underwater concrete that would not crack or dissolve in water was developed for the bridge's foundations. The concrete was mixed on a barge and then poured into the central chamber of the caissons continuously for three days and three nights. The water inside the caissons was gradually displaced, forced out by the thick mass of liquid concrete. To complete the operation, the hollow walls of each caisson were filled with concrete, together with steel bars for extra reinforcement.

A Structure Built for Stability

IN JANUARY 1990 six months after the caissons were installed, foundation work began for the bridge's mighty anchorages. On the Awaji side, solid granite lay just sixty-nine feet (21 m) below the surface. Because the depth was not too great, excavation was relatively easy. To support the surrounding soil while they dug, workers drove a circle of steel pipes into the ground to make a retaining wall. When they reached granite, they filled the excavation with concrete on top of the firm rock to complete the foundation.

The Kobe side presented more of a problem. With no solid rock below the surface, the work crew had to dig two hundred feet (61 m) below sea level to make a strong foundation. To support the sides of the excavation, they constructed a slurry wall nearly 280 feet (85 m) in diameter and seven feet (2.2 m) thick. A

Opposite:
Because of a new, high-strength wire made of silicon and steel, only two main cables were needed to suspend the bridge.

The anchorage bodies were topped with huge steel supporting frames to hold the main suspension cables.

slurry wall is used to dig deep foundations. First, a mechanical digger makes a deep trench, which is kept full of slurry to block groundwater from entering the excavation. Next, a metal cage is lowered into the hole to add reinforcement, and then concrete is poured in to displace the slurry. Finally, the concrete hardens to form a deep enclosed wall where workers can dig in safety. When the Kobe side excavation was finished, it too was filled with concrete. The colossal Kobe anchorage foundation is the largest bridge foundation in the world.

The anchorage bodies were made of reinforced concrete, using a specially developed highly fluid concrete. Ordinary concrete is made from rocks, sand, and water mixed with cement. Concrete is very strong when compressed but will crack if placed under tension, or pulling forces. To make reinforced concrete, steel bars or rods are encased inside the concrete while it is wet. This strengthens the concrete and makes it able to resist tension forces. The anchorage bodies were completed with huge steel supporting frames to anchor the strands of the main suspension cables.

The World's Tallest Bridge Towers

With the anchorages and caissons in place, work started on the towers in mid-1992. At 928 feet (282.8 m) high, the towers are taller than those of any other bridge. Each tower leg consists of thirty horizontal tiers, and each apartment-size tier is composed of three 32-foot-high (10 m) sections, like a row of hollow steel blocks. The sections were made in factories and then carried by barge to the tower base. Each one was carefully manufactured to exactly the right size to ensure the slightly tapered towers would be perfectly straight.

The tower sections were hoisted by a climbing, or boot-strapping, crane and then bolted into place. Perched on top of the unfinished tower, the crane pulled up each steel section and set it in place, then jacked itself up one level at a time as the tower grew. The tower legs are cross-shaped, like a tall column of stacked rectangular blocks with all four corners cut out, because wind tunnel tests showed that towers with flat, square surfaces may twist and bend under a strong wind. To

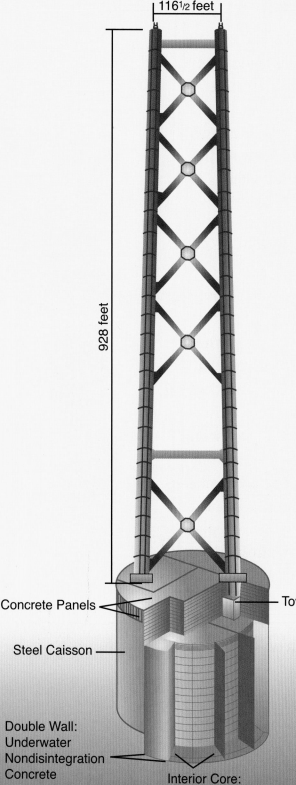

116½ feet

928 feet

Concrete Panels

Steel Caisson

Tower Anchor Frame

Double Wall:
Underwater
Nondisintegration
Concrete

Interior Core:
Nondisintegration Concrete

Main Tower Foundation

further protect the towers against wind, twenty tuned mass dampers were installed inside each one. Eight of the ten-ton pendulum-like weights were placed at the 690-foot (210 m) level, to damp sideways movements, with another twelve at the 590-foot (180 m) level, to damp twisting motions. Inside, the towers were divided into 102 floors, with an elevator at the center for easy maintenance.

A New Concept in Cables

The next task was to string the cables between the anchorages and over the towers, across almost two and a half miles (4 km) of ocean. Because the bridge construction could not block the crowded shipping channel, the cables could not be carried to the tower base by boat and then hoisted to the top of the towers, as was usually

done. Instead, in November 1993, the operation was carried out by helicopter. The helicopter carried light, strong pilot ropes, one attached to each of the anchorages, across the strait. The helicopter was used to place the ropes over the tower tops, and workers guided them into position. Next, stronger, heavier ropes were attached to the pilot ropes at one end and were winched across to the other side. When the stronger ropes had replaced the light pilot ropes, workers built a catwalk from prefabricated sections of planking and metal and suspended it from the ropes. They used this as a platform to string the huge main cables.

A new, high-strength wire made from a mix of steel and silicon was developed to make the main cables for the Akashi Kaikyo Bridge. Because the new wire was 12.5 percent stronger than the strongest wire used in earlier bridges, only two cables were needed

A helicopter was used to carry pilot ropes across the towers to begin the process of stringing the cables between the anchorages.

instead of the originally planned four. The gigantic twin cables contained 186,000 miles (300,000 km) of wire—enough to circle the earth seven and a half times.

Each 3.7-foot-thick (1.1 m) cable was made from 290 parallel strands. The factory-made strands, each containing 127 one-quarter-inch-thick wires bundled

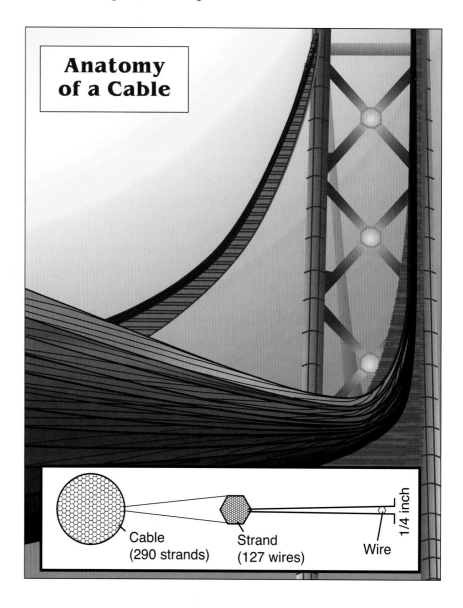

Anatomy of a Cable

Cable
(290 strands)

Strand
(127 wires)

1/4 inch

Wire

Each strand of the two huge cables was pulled individually over each tower top from one anchorage to the other.

together, were transported to the construction site on spools. Workers then pulled each strand individually from one anchorage to the other, over the saddle on each tower top. When all 290 strands were secured to the opposite anchorage, the crew used a machine to squeeze them together to form the main cables.

Earthquake!

Work to compress the cables was still in progress when disaster struck. At 5:46 A.M. on January 17, 1995, a 7.2-magnitude earthquake thundered through the city of Kobe. Buildings disintegrated and crashed to the ground. Fires raged. Approximately fifty-five hundred people were killed.

Engineers had designed the Akashi Kaikyo Bridge to withstand an 8.5-magnitude earthquake with an epicenter one hundred miles (161 km) away. The epicenter of the 1995 earthquake, called the Great Hanshin Earthquake, was just two and a half miles (4 km) from the construction site. It seemed impossible that the bridge could have escaped undamaged.

The Living Earth

Japan sits at one of the world's worst natural-disaster areas. Earthquakes are common, and Japan has more than 250 volcanoes, many still active. Undersea volcanoes and earthquakes often cause destructive tidal waves, or tsunamis, that flood coastal areas.

The vast forces that constantly threaten Japan are part of the process that created it. Like a gigantic puzzle, the earth's surface is composed of eight large and a few dozen smaller plates of rock. Japan lies where four of these plates meet and grind together. Millions of years ago, the Asian and Pacific plates collided and buckled, pushing up a chain of underwater mountains. The tips of the mountains rose above the ocean, and Japan was born.

Rocks still move continually at the plate boundaries. This activity can cause rock to melt or break, and Japan experiences many volcanic eruptions, as well as about fifteen hundred earthquakes each year. Many earth tremors are slight, but in 1923 the Kanto earthquake killed 143,000 people and devastated 70 percent of the city of Tokyo. On January 17, 1995, highways twisted and buildings collapsed

A giant crane pulls crushed cars out of debris after a 7.2 magnitude earthquake killed more than six thousand people in Kobe in 1995.

when the Great Hanshin earthquake struck the city of Kobe. Thousands of people were injured and fifty-five hundred died, many of them crushed to death under their fallen homes. The quake measured 7.2 on the Richter scale. It released as much energy as 44 billion pounds (20 billion kg) of TNT, or enough to heat New York City for one year.

The Japanese government spends billions of yen annually on earthquake research. Scientists and other experts use high-tech equipment to try to predict when another major earthquake will strike.

To the relief of everyone involved, though, the structure appeared intact. However, measurements revealed that the Awaji tower and anchorage had moved. "We frankly didn't believe it,"[1] said cable-work project manager Hajime Hosokawa. A week of surveys and frantic calculations showed that the rocks supporting the foundations had indeed moved, but the foundations themselves were not damaged. Construction stopped for a month while engineers decided how the bridge's design would be affected by this shift of the rock plates beneath the strait.

The structure of the bridge was not damaged. But something had changed—the drape of the cables. When the anchorage and tower had moved backward, the cables had lifted a little—just as a string held loosely between two hands will begin to lift in the middle if the person holding the string moves one end outward. The great curve of the main cables had become more than four feet (1.3 m) more shallow than before. The hangers, or suspender cables to hold the road deck, had already been manufactured. But because the main cables now hung slightly higher, the hangers would be a little too short. Rather than manufacture new hangers, the engineers decided to rework the tress sections so that the deck would rise a little higher. Along with the decreased cable sag, the earthquake had increased the bridge's center span by 2.6 feet (0.8 m) and the span on the Awaji side by almost one foot (0.3 m). The longest bridge in the world had just become even longer.

Chapter 4

The Bridge Is Completed

THE FINAL WORK to complete the Akashi Kaikyo Bridge proceeded swiftly. In June 1995, workers began to erect the truss girders that would support the six-lane road deck. The girders were made from relatively light, high-strength steel, but the bridge was so enormous that even so they contain ninety thousand tons of steel.

The truss sections were manufactured in a factory and transported to the bridge site. Workers used a huge floating crane to install the first preassembled sections at the towers and anchorages. Each of these initial sections was 116.5 feet (35.5 m) wide, forty-six feet (14 m) deep, and as long as a football field. Because the weight of a suspension bridge is transmitted to the foundations and anchorages by the main cables, the truss sections were not attached to the towers themselves. The crane hoisted the sections

Opposite:
The enormous bridge contains more than 193,000 tons of steel.

into position between the twin columns of each tower, where they were attached to hanger cables that hung vertically from the main cables. At each anchorage, the end of the highway approach road was connected to the first truss section of the bridge with a giant hinge, which would allow vertical movement of the bridge deck. The crew then worked inward from the towers and anchorages to bolt smaller sections one by one to the unfinished ends of the deck, above the deep, gray-blue waters of the strait. The truss erection proceeded equally from both towers and anchorages to ensure that the weight of the unfinished sections would always be balanced equally along the suspension cables.

The bridge authority could not use floating cranes to erect more than the first sections, as this would have disrupted ship traffic in the strait. Instead, barges took each forty-six-foot-square (14 m) unit to the base of the towers. Cranes, mounted high above on the truss, lifted each section up to the deck. Wheeled carts then rolled them to the end of the working face, where another crane lowered them into position. Finally, suspender cables were fixed onto each newly attached section for support. Vertical stabilizer plates were bolted beneath the center median on the main span truss to direct the wind and prevent dangerous waves of motion from forming.

To keep workers safe, the truss work often had to wait while winds stronger than thirty-six miles (58 km) per hour pounded the bridge. "Site work could proceed only on about 60 percent of normal work days,"[2]

said truss-erection project manager Ikuto Hara. In spite of the wind, the work went quickly, and in September 1996, the last section was bolted into place. Because strict safety precautions were followed at all times, not one worker was killed during the construction of the bridge. During the next eighteen months, the bridge was painted and the road surface paved. After ten years of construction work, the world's longest bridge was complete.

A huge floating crane installed the preassembled truss girders that support the roadway.

A Grand Opening

On April 4, 1998, an evening lighting ceremony transformed the Akashi Kaikyo Bridge into a fairy-tale sweep of lights. The next morning, Crown Prince Naruhito and his wife, Crown Princess Masako, cut a

The open triangles of the bridge's steel trusses make the bridge stable by reducing wind resistance.

ribbon to declare the bridge officially open. Buddhist priests blessed the bridge, and a representative from the U.S. Federal Highway Administration presented a letter of congratulation to the director of the Honshu-Shikoku Bridge Authority.

When the six-lane toll bridge opened to traffic later the same day, 5,350 cars crossed in the first hour. Instead of the sometimes perilous ferry journey between Kobe and Awaji Island, travelers could now choose a safe, five-minute drive for a one-way toll of twenty-six hundred yen—about nineteen U.S. dollars.

Although the Akashi Kaikyo Bridge was finally open, the responsibilities of the bridge authority did

not end. The first of the three links between Honshu and Shikoku, the Kojima-Sakaide route, had opened in 1988 for both road and rail traffic. The Kobe-Naruto route, which comprises the Akashi Kaikyo Bridge and the Ohnaruto Bridge between Awaji Island and Shikoku, was the second to open. As soon as the third link—the Onomichi-Imabari route—opened in 1999, the bridge authority founded the Long-Span Bridge Engineering Center. Its main task would be to maintain the eighteen bridges across the Seto Inland Sea, from one tiny island to another, to connect the two main islands.

Support Systems

To be sure the Akashi Kaikyo Bridge remains safe, information is constantly collected and analyzed. Automatic systems measure how many vehicles pass across the bridge and check traffic speed. TV monitors, emergency telephones, and traffic patrols ensure that traffic problems are detected and handled as quickly as possible. Displays along the bridge keep drivers informed of wind speed and transmit other safety information.

In addition to traffic movement, other factors that may affect the bridge are carefully monitored. Instruments mounted on the bridge include a seismograph to detect earthquake waves, an anemometer to measure wind speed, and accelerometers to measure motion. A global positioning system monitors the daily, hourly, and seasonal behavior of the bridge and tracks any changes caused by temperature or the weight of traffic. A weather observation system collects information on air temperature, road temperature, wind direction and speed, visibility, and rainfall.

The bridge structure has been protected from damage by rust and other corrosion. The gray-green paint, chosen to blend in with the city landscape, was a newly developed variety rich in zinc designed to resist corrosion. To protect the main cables, dry air is injected through a special system of pipes. This removes any moisture that might damage the cables from within. Inspection windows allow maintenance workers to view inside the protective casing that encloses the cables to check for possible damage. A ground-controlled magnetic device equipped with wheels, TV cameras, and a robotic arm is used to inspect the bridge coating, to touch up paint, and to make repairs.

A Pathway to the Future

Nationally, the gigantic highway project has simplified travel considerably. Before Japan's engineers bridged the Seto Inland Sea, about 290 scheduled ferryboat services were canceled each year due to bad weather. Since the Honshu-Shikoku bridges opened, the highway routes have closed an average of only 1.2 times per year. "The Honshu-Shikoku bridges reduced the traveling time between Honshu and Shikoku to one-third compared to using the previously existing ferry system,"[3] says Hiroyuki Fujikawa, president of the Honshu-Shikoku Bridge Authority.

The Akashi Kaikyo Bridge has dramatically increased the flow of people and goods between Honshu, Awaji, and Shikoku. Trucking companies can now

deliver goods between the islands on a reliable schedule. Fresh foods that would spoil when ferries were delayed can now be transported even when the ocean is too rough for boat travel. Thanks to the Honshu-Shikoku bridges, Shikoku companies can distribute their products easily to all parts of the nation. Many have increased production and expanded to new markets at much greater distances. New factories have been built on Shikoku, including an automobile factory. Several large retail stores have also been opened. No longer isolated, Japan's smallest main island has become a fast-growing part of the nation's economy.

The Akashi Kaikyo Bridge (background) makes it easy and safe to transport rice directly from paddies on Awaji to the four main islands of Japan.

The Akashi Kaikyo Bridge, a source of national pride for the Japanese, is a popular destination for tourists to Japan.

Tourism has flourished on Awaji and Shikoku. The Akashi Kaikyo Bridge itself has become a worldwide tourist attraction, with an exhibition center and a science museum that explains the technology used in the construction of the bridge. A 1,040-foot-long (317 m) walkway leads inside the girders of the bridge, from which visitors can gaze far down at the waters of the Akashi Strait—waters that engineers once believed too wide and deep to be bridged.

With 50 million cubic feet (1.42 million cubic meters) of concrete in its foundations and anchorages, and 193,200 tons of steel in its superstructure, the Akashi Kaikyo Bridge is an astounding feat of national engineering. It has brought growth and prosperity to a once-remote region and forms a vital link in the gigantic highway program that has united Japan's main islands for the first time in the nation's history.

Notes

Chapter Three: A Structure Built for Stability

1. Quoted in Dennis Normile, "Spanning Japan's Inland Sea," *Engineering News-Record*, vol. 237 no. 19, November 4, 1996, p. 33.

Chapter Four: The Bridge Is Completed

2. Quoted in Normile, "Spanning Japan's Inland Sea," p. 32.
3. Honshu-Shikoku Bridge Authority brochure. *Honshu-Shikoku Bridges—Steps to the 21st Century.*

For More Information

Books

Jan Adkins, *Bridges: From My Side to Yours.* Brookfield, CT: Roaring Book Press, 2002.

David J. Brown, *Bridges.* New York: Macmillan, 1993.

Jen Green, *Japan.* Austin: Steck-Vaughn, 2001.

Ann Heinrichs, *Japan.* New York: Childrens Press, 1998.

Web Sites

History of the Honshu-Shikoku Bridge Project (www.rpi.edu/~brawi/frame_ft_jbt/bridgepic18a.htm). Explains the history and planning of the Akashi Kaikyo Bridge, with details of how its various components were built.

Honshu-Shikoku Bridge Authority (www.hsba.go.jp/bridge/e-akasi.htm). Official Web site of the Honshu-Shikoku Bridge Authority.

Chronology

1853	Captain Matthew Perry convinces Japan to allow trade with other countries. This begins a process of modernization and development for the Japanese nation.
1940	Inspired by California's Golden Gate Bridge, government public works manager Chujiro Haraguchi proposes a technical plan to build a bridge from Shikoku to Awaji Island. World War II halts construction plans.
1950	The Japanese government passes the National Land Comprehensive Development Law to help develop remote parts of the country and encourage economic growth.
1955	A ferry collision between Honshu and Shikoku highlights the need for a bridge. The Japan National Railway and the Japanese Ministry of Construction begin studies for possible road and rail links between Honshu and Shikoku.
1967	The Japan Society of Civil Engineers technical committee presents a report in favor of a road project for three routes to link Honshu and Shikoku.
1970	The Honshu-Shikoku Bridge Authority is created.
1986	Ground-breaking ceremony for the Akashi Kaikyo Bridge.
1988	On-site construction begins.
1989	Caissons are installed.
1990	Work begins for anchorage foundations.
1992	Erection of towers begins; anchorage foundations completed.
1993	Tower erection completed; pilot ropes are put in place by helicopter.
1994	Cables are erected.
1995	The Great Hanshin Earthquake devastates Kobe and moves the Awaji tower and anchorage, increasing the total length of the bridge by 3.6 feet. Erection work on stiffening trusses begins.
1996	Truss work is completed.
1997	Pavement of road deck begins.
1998	Akashi Kaikyo Bridge opens to traffic.

Glossary

abutment—The end support of an arch bridge, built on the bank, to support the outward thrusting forces of the arch.

anchorages—Huge onshore support structures to anchor the ends of the cables of a suspension bridge.

caisson—A cylindrical shell used to make underwater foundations.

center span—The middle section of a suspension bridge, measured between its two support towers.

compression—The force that presses things together and shortens them.

hanger cables—Cables that hang from the curved main cables of a suspension bridge to hold up the road deck. They are also called suspender cables.

reinforced concrete—Concrete strengthened with steel bars to give it strength under tension, or pulling forces.

tension—The force that pulls things apart or lengthens them.

truss—A supporting frame made of connected triangles used to strengthen bridge decks.

tsunami—A giant wave caused by underwater volcanoes or earthquakes. Sometimes called tidal waves, tsunamis can be up to one hundred feet high and travel 450 miles per hour.

tuned mass dampers—Huge, pendulum-like devices mounted in bridge towers to prevent motion caused by wind.

typhoon—A tropical hurricane with a wind speed of seventy-four miles per hour or more.

Index